1 9 8 9
The Year You Were Born

Birth Certificate

Name: _____

Birthdate: _____

Time: _____

Place of Birth: _____

Weight: _____ Length: _____

Mother's name: _____

Father's name: _____

D1472762

For Dashiell Lunde from his Auntie Jeanne—J.M.

To Caitlin Horton with love from Aunt Judy—J.L.

ISBN 0-688-14386-5 (pbk.)   ISBN 0-688-14385-7 (lib. bdg.)

1 3 5 7 9 10 8 6 4 2
First edition

1989

The Year You Were Born

Compiled by

JEANNE MARTINET

Illustrated by

JUDY LANFREDI

Tambourine Books · New York

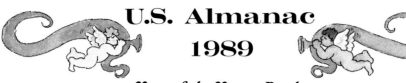

U.S. Almanac
1989

Year of the Young Reader

President George Bush

Population 248,762,000
Males 121,445,000
Females 127,317,000

Number of Births
Boys 2,069,000
Girls 1,971,000

Average weight at birth 7 pounds, 7 ounces

Cost of baby's first year $5,774

Most popular baby girl's name
Ashley

Most popular baby boy's name
Michael

Number of Deaths 2,150,000

Tornadoes 856

Top Crop Corn, 191,000,000 metric tons

Most snow
246.3 inches in Marquette, Michigan

Most rain
67.46 inches in New Orleans, Louisiana

Highest temperature Phoenix, Arizona, 118°F

Households with TV sets 90,000,000

Households with VCRs 58,000,000

Favorite TV show The Cosby Show

Amount of TV kids age 6–11 watch
19 hours, 38 minutes per week

Top movie (highest earnings)
Batman, $251,000,000

Number of children's books sold
281,000,000

Number of daily newspapers published 1,626

Favorite food
Red meat, 135.4 pounds per person

Favorite dinner for kids age 6–14 Pizza

Number of Boy Scouts 4,247,000

Number of Girl Scouts 2,415,000

Favorite sport for kids age 7–11 Swimming

Number of grandparents 54,000,000

Number of words in the written vocabulary of kids 6–14
About 10,000

Amount of trash thrown out
1,300 pounds per person

Americans who believe in ghosts 25%

Top pet Cat, population 57,900,000

Pieces of U.S. mail delivered throughout world
161,603,000,000

January

*J*anuary is named after Janus, the Roman god of doorways and of beginnings.

BIRTHSTONE *Garnet*

SUNDAY
January 1

New Year's Day • More than 100 hot-air balloons take off from 98 cities all over France to launch the year-long celebration of the 200th anniversary of the French Revolution.

MONDAY
January 2

Doctors in Tucson, Arizona, perform a heart bypass operation on Marjorie Rorabough, who received a new heart 10 years ago. It's the first operation of this kind on a transplant patient.

TUESDAY
January 3

A 40-foot-tall 4,200-pound gorilla statue at the Wild Water Rapids Water Park in Virginia Beach, Virginia, burns up. No one knows how it caught fire.

WEDNESDAY
January 4

Off the coast of New South Wales, Australia, dolphins save the life of a 17-year-old surfer when they chase away a large shark that is attacking him. The shark had already bitten a large piece off his surfboard!

Get lost, shark breath!

THURSDAY
January 5

Snow falls in the Khūr desert in Iran for the first time in 50 years. • A 5,400-pound Bryde's whale that beached itself in Orlando, Florida, is returned to the Gulf of Mexico.

FRIDAY
January 6

FIZZ WHIZZES: Students at Clarkson University have built about 35 small cars—each powered by 12 Alka-Seltzer tablets!

PLOP! PLOP!

CLARKSON CU

SATURDAY
January 7

President Ronald Reagan has surgery to straighten his crooked left ring finger. • A tornado hits Allendale, Illinois.

SUNDAY
January 8

A company in Wellesley, Massachusetts, is selling contact lenses for chickens! The red lenses, which are said to make chickens calmer, cost 15 cents a pair.

MONDAY
January 9

Scientists at Bristol University in England begin tests on a 40,000-year-old piece of mammoth skin from the Soviet Union. Mammoths were prehistoric elephants.

WHO ELSE WAS BORN IN JANUARY?
OPRAH WINFREY

U.S. entertainer
Oprah Winfrey's national TV talk show has won 3
Emmy Awards. In 1986, she was nominated for
an Academy Award for her role of Sophia in the
movie *The Color Purple.*
BORN   January 29, 1954, in Kosciusko, Mississippi

TUESDAY
January 10

An international team of scientists reports that a 90-trillion-mile-long stream of gas is flowing toward the center of the Milky Way, into what may be a black hole.

WEDNESDAY
January 11

At a special conference in Paris, France, 149 nations agree not to use chemical weapons.

THURSDAY
January 12

In Atlanta, Georgia, a man named Frank Argenbright has offered local elementary students free bicycles if they improve their school attendance, grades, and behavior.

FRIDAY
January 13

The world's oldest twins celebrate their 105th birthday. They are Allie Hill and Maggie Lambeth, of Denton, North Carolina.

SATURDAY
January 14

Helicopters rescue 32 people from a 42,000-ton aircraft carrier called the *Yarrawonga,* which is sinking off the west coast of Ireland.

SUNDAY
January 15

The Mexican navy helps free 31 pilot whales stranded in the Bay of La Paz off the Baja California peninsula.

MONDAY
January 16

Martin Luther King Day • 10 snakes, 2 iguanas, and a $1,400 cockatoo are stolen from 2 pet shops in Nassau County, New York.

TUESDAY
January 17

In Fontana, California, a clumsy crook steals $2,900 from a bank and then accidentally drops it before he runs away. The wind blows the money into the hands of people passing by; all but $20 is returned to the bank.

BIRTHDAYS IN 1989

U.S. Congress 200 Years

The Electric Clock 150 Years

Nylon Stockings 50 Years

The Jukebox 100 Years

TV Broadcasting 50 Years

The Electric Sewing Machine 100 Years

Little League 50 Years

The Steam Shovel 150 Years

The Eiffel Tower 100 Years

Barbie Dolls 30 Years

Pay Phones 100 Years

The Hamburger 100 Years

Batman 50 Years

WEDNESDAY
January 18

Astronomers in Chile discover a pulsar that rotates 2,000 times each second—faster than any other ever found. The pulsar is so dense that one teaspoon of it would weigh 300,000 tons on earth!

THURSDAY
January 19

On display at the Housewares Exhibition in Chicago, Illinois: a new kind of baby bottle that turns white if the milk is too hot.

FRIDAY
January 20

George Bush is sworn in as the 41st President of the United States in Washington, D.C. The Inauguration Day Parade features 98 floats. • In San Antonio, Texas, the George Club meets; all its members are named George.

SATURDAY
January 21

Full Moon

George and Barbara Bush open the White House to several thousand visitors. • 10 paintings, including 2 by Grandma Moses, are stolen from an art gallery in Boston, Massachusetts.

SUNDAY
January 22

Super Bowl XXIII is won by the San Francisco 49ers, who defeat the Cincinnati Bengals 20–16. During the game, millions of people watch the world's first 3-D TV commercial, for Coca-Cola.

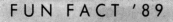

FUN FACT '89

There are approximately 423,618,800 telephones in the world.

| MONDAY
January 23 | The sun finally comes up at 1:09 P.M. in Barrow, Alaska, after 65 days of darkness. The long night is due to the earth's tilt in relation to the sun during this part of the year. |

| TUESDAY
January 24 | In Milwaukee, Wisconsin, teams from 14 countries begin turning 10-ton blocks of ice into works of art at the U.S. International Snow Sculpting Competition. |

| WEDNESDAY
January 25 | A huge fireball streaks across the sky in the northeastern U.S. Experts believe it is a meteor. |

| THURSDAY
January 26 | Hundreds of cowboys recite poetry and sing songs at the Cowboy Poetry Gathering in Elko, Nevada. |

| FRIDAY
January 27 | 16 right whales have been spotted off the coasts of Florida and Georgia, which is a good sign for this endangered species. |

| SATURDAY
January 28 | Alaska is having its worst cold wave ever. The temperature today in Nome is −54°F, the coldest recorded since people started keeping track in 1906. |

| SUNDAY
January 29 | The Soviet spacecraft *Phobos 2,* which was launched last year, goes into orbit around Mars. • In Clarksville, Missouri, Omega the trained eagle performs at the Eagle Day Festival. |

| MONDAY
January 30 | Egyptian archaeologists discover 5 life-sized granite statues dating from 1470 B.C. near the Temple of Luxor in Egypt. |

| TUESDAY
January 31 | A Greenpeace boat called the *Gondwana* runs into a Japanese whaling boat off the coast of Antarctica. Protestors on board the *Gondwana* are trying to block the Japanese from harpooning minke whales. |

JAPAN'S EMPEROR HIROHITO DIES AT 87

POLICE CHASE 8-YEAR-OLD BOY DRIVING CAR

1,000 STUDENTS DEMAND GRADES FROM TEACHERS ON STRIKE IN LOS ANGELES

EARTHQUAKE SHAKES UTAH

February

*T*he name February comes from the Latin *februa*, which means "feast of purification."

BIRTHSTONE *Amethyst*

WEDNESDAY
February 1

FRUIT FLASH: Officials report that the chemical daminozide, which is used on 5% of America's apples, can be harmful to humans.

THURSDAY
February 2

Groundhog Day • Groundhog Punxsutawney Phil of Pennsylvania sees his shadow, which means 6 more weeks of winter, but groundhogs General Lee of Atlanta, Chipper of Chicago, and Melvin of Greensboro, North Carolina, don't see theirs. In Irvington, Kentucky, Ted the rooster just walks around in circles!

FRIDAY
February 3

BARK BREAK: A veterinarian named Bonnie Beaver has invented a bark-stopping electronic dog collar. When the collar "hears" barking, it gives off a special sound that quiets the dog.

SATURDAY
February 4

On this day in 1877, the empress of Brazil presented the queen of England with a dress woven of spiderwebs.

SUNDAY
February 5

Maria Waliser of Switzerland wins the women's Alpine downhill skiing world championship in Vail, Colorado.

MONDAY
February 6

A runaway train carrying coal derails in Colorado Springs, Colorado. 64 of the 66 cars are knocked off the track.
• Hansjoerg Tauscher of West Germany wins the men's Alpine downhill skiing world championship.

TUESDAY
February 7

A 60-year-old woman in Merritt Island, Florida, chains herself to an oak tree in front of her home to try to save it from being cut down to make way for a road.

WEDNESDAY
February 8

15-year-old Jeffrey Scott Campbell of Denver, Colorado, wins Nintendo's Invent the Ultimate Video Game contest. His game is called "Lockarm" and features a 6-armed king named Okra.

WHO ELSE WAS BORN IN FEBRUARY?
ROSA PARKS

U.S civil rights leader
On December 1, 1955, she started the famous bus boycott in Montgomery, Alabama, by refusing to give up her seat to a white man. Her courageous act marked the beginning of an organized civil rights movement.
BORN   February 4, 1913, in Tuskegee, Alabama

THURSDAY
February 9

The annual race up the stairs of 86 floors of the Empire State Building is won by 2 Australians: Robin Rishworth (men's), in 11 minutes, 9 seconds, and Suzanne Malaxos (women's), in a record-breaking 12 minutes, 25 seconds.

FRIDAY
February 10

UFO ALERT: In Fyffe, Alabama, a strange light is seen in the sky. Police report a large, unidentified flying object passing over the town.

SATURDAY
February 11

Barbara Harris becomes the first female bishop in the Episcopal Church.

SUNDAY
February 12

Lincoln's birthday • At the Inventor's Expo in Crystal City, Virginia, new inventions are demonstrated, including an automatic transmission for bicycles and a hammer that won't let you smash your thumb.

MONDAY
February 13

Barbie turns 30! A huge party is thrown for the famous Mattel doll in New York City. • A small iron meteor crashes through the roof of a train station in Sussex, England.

TUESDAY
February 14

Valentine's Day • 2,628 dogs enter the Westminster Kennel Club Show in New York City. The winner: a red Doberman female whose official name is Ch. Royal Tudor's Wild as the Wind, C.D., but who is called "Indy."

WEDNESDAY
February 15

A black Alaskan timber wolf chews through his wooden crate and escapes from the National Zoo in Washington, D.C.

THURSDAY
February 16

WHAT A DOLL: A blue-eyed doll made in Germany in 1909 is sold at Sotheby's in London, England, for more than $140,000!

CHINESE YEAR OF THE SNAKE
February 6, 1989–January 26, 1990

Chinese horoscopes follow a 12-year cycle. According to legend, Buddha summoned all the animals in the world to him one New Year, promising them a reward. Only 12 obeyed, and he gave them each a year; the Rat arrived first so he got the first year! The order is always the same: Rat, Ox, Tiger, Hare, Dragon, Snake, Horse, Sheep, Monkey, Rooster, Dog, and Pig.

People born in the year of the Snake can be quiet and slow on the outside, but fiery and active on the inside. They tend to be cautious and like to keep things hidden. Snakes are usually very patient and very smart, but can be moody. They love music, theater, and dance, and they like to sleep a lot. Snakes get along well with Dragons and Dogs, but *not* with Tigers, Pigs, Hares, or Sheep.

Some famous Snakes: Clarence Darrow, Grete Waitz, Clara Barton, Mahatma Gandhi, Indira Gandhi, Jesse Jackson, Howard Hughes, Martha Graham, Anne Frank, John F. Kennedy, John Hancock, Johannes Brahms, Nicolaus Copernicus, Bob Dylan, Greta Garbo, Henri Matisse, Jacqueline Kennedy Onassis, and Pablo Picasso.

FRIDAY
February 17

Archaeologists in Israel have found a 2,000-year-old jug with 2,000-year-old perfume in it. The jug was buried in a 3-foot-deep pit in a cave near the Dead Sea and was wrapped in palm leaves. The oil is from the ancient persimmon plant, which is now extinct.

SATURDAY
February 18

Helicopters and boats rescue 175 people trapped on a 1-mile-long piece of ice in Lake Erie. They had been ice fishing when the huge piece of ice broke off and started floating away.

SUNDAY
February 19

Happy birthday, Batman! He first appeared in *Detective Comics* on this day in 1939.

MONDAY
February 20

Full Moon

Tonight a total eclipse of the moon can be seen from the western half of North America.
• A man named Joseph Wheelwright has invented a three-wheel roller skate.

TUESDAY
February 21

The Soviet Union's *Phobos 2* spacecraft sends back the first 9 pictures of Mars's moon Phobos.

FUN FACT '89
Barbie dolls are sold in 67 countries; a Barbie doll is bought every 2 seconds.

WEDNESDAY
February 22

Washington's birthday • Mickey Mouse has a new set of wheels at Walt Disney World in Florida. The 40-foot-long car is called a "li-mouse-ine" and has a Tinkerbell hood ornament—and a fully stocked cheese cabinet inside!

THURSDAY
February 23

2 men wearing ski masks steal $2,000,000 in gold from a safe in a gold merchant's office in New York City. • Warning: Medical experts say mumps is on the rise.

FRIDAY
February 24

The body of Emperor Hirohito of Japan is entombed in a mausoleum after a 13-hour funeral ceremony in Tokyo. • The governor of Maine marries one of Maine's U.S. representatives.

SATURDAY
February 25

The annual Festival of Whales begins at Dana Point, California. Thousands of people line the shores to watch gray whales migrating to the Arctic from Baja California. • In the Netherlands, Igor Zhelozovsky of the U.S.S.R. breaks the 1,000-meter speed skating record in 1 minute, 12.58 seconds.

SUNDAY
February 26

Argentine and American inventors have created a sonic fishing lure that uses sound waves to attract the fish. The lure acts like a dinner bell.

MONDAY
February 27

A crowd of 49,908 people shows up at the Livestock Show and Rodeo in Houston, Texas. That's a new world record for attendance at a rodeo.

TUESDAY
February 28

78-year-old snake expert William Haast is bitten by a venomous Pakistani pit viper. It's the 149th time he has been bitten by a snake.

KING OF MOROCCO BECOMES FIRST MONARCH TO RECEIVE U.S. PATENT

JULIE THE HIPPO FROM MEMPHIS HAS TWINS

ICE CREAM FOR DOGS GOES ON SALE

SKIER RUNS INTO DEER ON A SLOPE IN VERMONT

March

*M*arch is named for the Roman god of war, Mars.

BIRTHSTONE *Aquamarine*

WEDNESDAY
March 1

The entire town of Bolan, Iowa, appears on the TV show *Late Night with David Letterman*. The town has a population of only 16 people!

THURSDAY
March 2

12 European countries agree to do away with chemicals that harm the earth's ozone layer by the year 2000.

FRIDAY
March 3

More than 4,000 people assemble in the town of Fyffe, Alabama, to try to catch a glimpse of the UFO seen on February 10. No aliens appear.

SATURDAY
March 4

Chow Tai Fook of Hong Kong buys a rough uncut diamond for the record high price of $10,000,000.

SUNDAY
March 5

Mild earthquakes shake parts of Arizona and Washington.
• Coweta, Georgia, is devastated by several violent tornadoes.

MONDAY
March 6

A large solar flare spouts on the surface of the sun, causing interference to shortwave radios over half of the earth. • More than 30 earthquakes rattle Imperial Valley, California.

NEAR DIS-ASTEROID!

Most people in the world don't even notice when a huge asteroid called 1989FC almost hits the earth on March 23. That's because although the encounter is a "near-miss" in space terms, 1989FC is still 430,000 miles away at its closest pass—about twice the distance between the earth and the moon.

1989FC is about 1,300 feet wide, is made of rock and dust, and is traveling at a speed of 46,000 miles an hour. If 1989FC had hit the earth, it would have made a crater up to 4 miles wide and would have caused the damage of 20,000 hydrogen bombs. An asteroid of this size runs into our planet about every 100,000 years. Some scientists believe that a much bigger asteroid hit Earth 65,000,000 years ago and helped wipe out the dinosaurs.

WHO ELSE WAS BORN IN MARCH?
MIKHAIL GORBACHEV

Russian political leader
He was secretary general of the national Communist
Party from 1985 until 1991. In 1988 he became
the official president of the Soviet Union. He
brought a new open-mindedness to the government
and won the Nobel Peace Prize in 1990.
BORN   March 21, 1931, in Privolye, Stavropol, Russia

TUESDAY
March 7

A partial eclipse of the sun can be seen from parts of the
Pacific, western North America, and Greenland. By 10:50 A.M.
(PST) the moon blocks about 40% of the sun.

WEDNESDAY
March 8

Radioactive steam leaks into the air from a nuclear power plant
near Charlotte, North Carolina. The reactor is shut down.

THURSDAY
March 9

Another huge solar flare, 36 times the size of the earth, erupts
from the sun, shooting about 70,000 miles into space. It's the
largest ever recorded.

FRIDAY
March 10

New York City is building 25 owl houses to put
in the city's parks. Officials are hoping that rat-eating
owls will move to the parks and help control the rat
population. An owl can kill 3 rats a night.

SATURDAY
March 11

3 more large solar flares. • Hemlock trees in New York,
Connecticut, and New Jersey are being killed by tiny insects
called woolly adelgids. The bugs look like small Q-Tips.

SUNDAY
March 12

On this day in 1912, Juliette Gordon Low founded the Girl
Scouts of America in Savannah, Georgia. They were called Girl
Guides.

MONDAY
March 13

U.S. space shuttle *Discovery* is launched from Cape Canaveral,
Florida, on a 5-day mission—with 5 astronauts, 4 rats, 32
fertilized hens' eggs, and a small garden of lilies and weeds.

TUESDAY
March 14

Firefighters battle wildfires in the grasslands of Texas. 44,000
acres have burned so far. • Dust storms in Kansas.

WEDNESDAY
March 15

In Alaska, Joe Runyan wins the 1158-mile Iditarod Trail Sled Dog Race. He and his dogs make it from Anchorage to Nome in just over 11 days, 5 hours.

THURSDAY
March 16

President Bush talks to the astronauts in space by telephone. The astronauts are studying incubating chicken eggs today.

FRIDAY
March 17

President Bush's English springer spaniel Millie gives birth to 6 puppies at the White House. • The world's oldest known mummy is discovered near the Great Pyramid of Cheops in Egypt. The mummy is that of a woman who was buried around 2600 B.C.

SATURDAY
March 18

Space shuttle *Discovery* lands at Edwards Air Force Base in California. • At California's Disneyland, 150 people are stuck 40 feet up in the air for 5 hours when the Skyway cable cars break down.

SUNDAY
March 19

At the Banana Slug Festival in Guerneville, California, a large yellow slug named Slimer wins the slug races.

MONDAY
March 20

Spring equinox • The annual Rotten Sneaker Championship is held in Montpelier, Vermont, to select the most rotten—but still wearable—pair of sneakers. The owner of the winning pair receives new sneakers and a trophy.

TUESDAY
March 21

Russian spacecraft *Phobos 2* reaches orbit around the Martian moon Phobos. • The first submarine-launched *Trident 2* missile spins out of control just 4 seconds after lift-off from the USS *Tennessee* near Cape Canaveral, Florida.

WEDNESDAY
March 22

Full Moon

The Hindu spring festival of Holi. • National Goof-off Day in the U.S.

THURSDAY
March 23

A huge asteroid whizzes past the earth, missing it by only 430,000 miles.

FUN FACT '89

The greater honeyguide in Africa is a bird that comes when you whistle and then leads you to a beehive.

FRIDAY	Supertanker *Exxon Valdez* runs aground in Prince William

FRIDAY
March 24

Supertanker *Exxon Valdez* runs aground in Prince William Sound in southeastern Alaska, causing the worst oil spill in U.S. history. 11,000,000 gallons of oil are dumped into the water.

SATURDAY
March 25

CARTOON CROOK: Valuable comic strips from the Museum of Cartoon Art in Rye Brook, New York, have been stolen, including some original Dick Tracy strips from 1944.

SUNDAY
March 26

Easter Sunday • A California condor at the San Diego Zoo lays an egg today! The egg is aqua, weighs 10 ounces, and is 5 inches long. There are only 28 California condors left in the world.

MONDAY
March 27

In Homer, Georgia, about 20,000 children search for 72,000 dyed hens' eggs and 68,000 candy eggs at the annual Garrison family Easter egg hunt.

TUESDAY
March 28

U.S.S.R. ground control has lost contact with the Soviet spacecraft *Phobos 2*. The mission is aborted. *Phobos 2* was scheduled to land on the Martian moon.

WEDNESDAY
March 29

Domingo Tan of Alexandria, Virginia, has invented an aerosol spray that instantly cools the interior of a car that has been sitting in the hot sun.

THURSDAY
March 30

SNEAKER SNEEZING: Researchers from 2 U.S. universities report that some people may be allergic to their sneakers, due to the irritating chemicals in the rubber of most athletic shoes.

FRIDAY
March 31

Deeanne Eggleston of Novato, California, who is almost completely blind, sets out from the Golden Gate Bridge for a 4-month bicycle trip to Washington, D.C. A friend rides ahead of her, wearing bright colors.

STORM ON THE SUN CAUSES ELECTRICITY TO FAIL IN QUEBEC

$7,000,000 DRESS WORN IN PARIS

NEW EARTHQUAKE RIDE OPENS AT UNIVERSAL STUDIOS IN HOLLYWOOD

FATHER AND SON CHESS PLAYERS DEFECT FROM SOVIET UNION

April

*T*he name April comes from the Latin *aperire,* which means "to open." April is known as the time of budding.

BIRTHSTONE *Diamond*

SATURDAY
April 1

First Lady Barbara Bush celebrates April Fools' Day by wearing a strawberry-blond wig at a party in Washington, D.C. • In Florida, a radio announcer tricks listeners into believing 35 whales are circling Key West.

SUNDAY
April 2

The NCAA women's college basketball championship is won by Tennessee, which defeats Auburn, 76–60.

MONDAY
April 3

Michigan beats Seton Hall, 80–79, in the NCAA men's college basketball championship. • An earthquake measuring 4.5 on the Richter scale cracks concrete and shatters windows in San Francisco.

TUESDAY
April 4

Because of the oil spill in Alaska, hundreds of oil-soaked birds and animals are being brought to an animal rescue center where their wounds are treated and the oil is washed from skin and feathers. They are allowed to rest, then released back into the wild.

WEDNESDAY
April 5

In Washington, D.C., President Bush presents a crystal apple to Mary Bicouvaris of Hampton, Virginia, and names her Teacher of the Year.

THURSDAY
April 6

SNAKE SNEAK: 3 constrictor snakes have been stolen from the zoo in Boise, Idaho. One of them is a 13-foot-long Burmese python and weighs 48 pounds.

FRIDAY
April 7

Soviet leader Mikhail Gorbachev has lunch with Queen Elizabeth at Windsor Castle near London.

SATURDAY
April 8

In Raymond, Illinois, the U.S. Postal Service throws a birthday party for the nation's longest serving postal employee, August Sutter, who started with the post office in 1929. He is 80 and still working!

WHO ELSE WAS BORN IN APRIL?
SONJA HENIE

Norwegian figure skater
A champion skater by age 14, she went on to win
10 consecutive women's world figure skating titles
(1927–1936), as well as Olympic gold medals in
1928, 1932, and 1936. From 1936 to 1945 she
starred in 10 Hollywood movies where she dazzled
audiences with her spectacular skill as a skating dancer.
BORN   April 8, 1912, in Oslo, Norway

SUNDAY
April 9

The most complicated watch in the world—a watch with
1,728 separate parts—is sold for a record high price of
$2,520,000 in Switzerland. It took jewelers 9 years to make
and even shows the position of the Milky Way.

MONDAY
April 10

A team of 122 people in Indonesia have made the tallest cake
in the world. It is 77 feet, 8 inches high. They began baking it
in February.

TUESDAY
April 11

The government of Kenya asks the rest of the world to stop all
trading of ivory, in order to try to save its country's dwindling
elephant population.

WEDNESDAY
April 12

A 9-foot piece of the tail of a Concorde jet carrying 95
passengers falls off during a flight to try to set an around-the-
world speed record. The plane, which was traveling 1,500
miles per hour at 44,000 feet, is forced to land.

THURSDAY
April 13

The Dinosaurs Live exhibition
opens at the Natural History
Museum in London, England—
complete with life-sized, computer-
controlled prehistoric monsters.

FRIDAY
April 14

The Chinese government reports that the population of China
has reached 1.1 billion—about 22 percent of the total
population of the world.

SATURDAY
April 15

David Goeddel, William Kohr, Diane Pennica, and Gordon
Vehar have been named Inventors of the Year for developing a
drug that dissolves blood clots in heart attack victims. The
drug is called TPA.

1989 AWARDS BOARD

Nobel Peace Prize: Tenzin Gyatso, the Dalai Lama of Tibet
National Teacher of the Year: Mary Bicouvaris of Hampton, Virginia
National Spelling Bee Champion: Scott Isaacs, Littleton, Colorado
Female Athlete of the Year: Steffi Graf, tennis
Male Athlete of the Year: Joe Montana, football
Horse of the Year: Sunday Silence
Best Movie (Academy Award): *Driving Miss Daisy*
Best Visual/Special Effects (Academy Award): *The Abyss*
Best album (Grammy Award): *Nick of Time* by Bonnie Raitt
Best single (Grammy Award): *Wind Beneath My Wings* by Bette Midler
Best children's book (Newbery Medal): *Joyful Noise: Poems for Two
   Voices* by Paul Fleischman
Best children's book illustration (Caldecott Medal): *Song and Dance Man*
   written by Karen Ackerman, illustrated by Stephen Gammell

SUNDAY
April 16

At the World Gold Panning Championship in Dahlonega, Georgia, Don Roberts breaks the world record when he pans 8 gold nuggets in a 10-inch-diameter pan in only 7.55 seconds.

MONDAY
April 17

The Boston Marathon is won by Abebe Mekonnen of Ethiopia in 2 hours, 9 minutes, 6 seconds. The women's race is won by Ingrid Kristiansen of Norway in 2 hours, 24 minutes, and 33 seconds.

TUESDAY
April 18

Happy 20th birthday to Princess Nori of Japan.
• Alligator hunter Columbus White has harpooned the biggest alligator ever caught in Florida; it's over 13 feet long and weighs 1,043 pounds.

WEDNESDAY
April 19

Passover begins at sundown. • An 18-foot-wide tostada is made in Hollywood, California, with 162 pounds of beans, 600 heads of lettuce, 40 pounds of sausage, and 40 pounds of grated cheese. It is mixed by a cement mixer! • A California condor chick is hatched at the San Diego Zoo. It is named Mandan.

THURSDAY
April 20

Full Moon

In Alaska, a huge Soviet oil skimmer joins U.S. efforts to clean up the worst U.S. oil spill in history. The Russian ship can sweep up 5,000 barrels of oil in one hour.

FRIDAY
April 21

66 cats are found in an apartment in Jersey City, New Jersey.
• Forest fires start in the Rocky Mountains in Colorado.

FUN FACT '89   California condors lay only 1 egg every 2 years.

SATURDAY *April 22*	Earth Day • A hot-air balloon called *Rainbow Endeavor* flies over the North Pole carrying the message SAVE THE OZONE LAYER. It floats at 1,000 feet and collects samples of Arctic air.
SUNDAY *April 23*	Sean Lomak wins the whistling championship at the National Whistlers Convention in Louisburg, North Carolina.
MONDAY *April 24*	In New York City, William Sokolin accidentally breaks a $500,000 bottle of 1787 Châteaux Margaux wine once owned by Thomas Jefferson. • Scientists have discovered a cure for hiccups: a drug called nifedipine.
TUESDAY *April 25*	Countdown begins for the launch of space shuttle *Atlantis*. • 10 to 15 members of a rare species of rhinoceros, called Java rhinoceros, have been discovered living in Vietnam.
WEDNESDAY *April 26*	In Pennsylvania, the numbers for the world's largest lotto jackpot—a whopping $115,000,000—are drawn tonight. 14 winning tickets split the prize.
THURSDAY *April 27*	3 Soviet cosmonauts touch down in Kazakhstan, Central Asia, from the orbiting space station *Mir,* leaving it empty for the first time in 2 years. • Buildings in Memphis, Tennessee, sway from an earthquake measuring 4.7 on the Richter scale.
FRIDAY *April 28*	The countdown for space shuttle *Atlantis* is stopped 31 seconds before launch because of a problem with an engine fuel line.
SATURDAY *April 29*	Archaeologists in Israel have dug up a 60,000-year-old skeleton that proves that Neanderthals had the bone structure needed for human speech.
SUNDAY *April 30*	To celebrate the 200th anniversary of the inauguration of George Washington, a 2-hour parade is held in New York City. An actor playing Washington reenacts the original swearing-in ceremony.

Nuclear Sub SINKS IN NORWEGIAN SEA

PRESIDENT BUSH DEDICATES NEW WHITE HOUSE HORSESHOE PIT

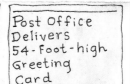

Post Office Delivers 54-Foot-high Greeting Card

JOHN LENNON'S MERCEDES BENZ SOLD FOR $211,500

May

*M*ay comes from Maia, who was the Roman goddess
of growth, increase, and blossoming.

BIRTHSTONE *Emerald*

MONDAY *May 1*	A brave train conductor leaps off a train near Ramsey, New Jersey, to save 2 small children who are playing on the tracks.
TUESDAY *May 2*	A thief breaks into the zoo in Albuquerque, New Mexico, and steals an Australian king parrot, a sulphur-crested cockatoo, and a dusky lory. • At the University of Iowa, 8 pigeons have been taught to recognize facial expressions!
WEDNESDAY *May 3*	Roscoe Mack of Orlando, Florida, is named Residential Garbage Man of the Year. • President Bush plays tennis with tennis star Bjorn Borg on the White House courts.
THURSDAY *May 4*	U.S. space shuttle *Atlantis* blasts off from Cape Canaveral, Florida, carrying the *Magellan* space probe, which is headed for Venus.
FRIDAY *May 5*	150 members of the American Roller Coaster Enthusiasts become the first people to ride the world's tallest, steepest, and fastest roller coaster, the Magnum XL-200 at the Cedar Point amusement park in Sandusky, Ohio. It is 201 feet tall, has a 60-degree angle, and reaches a speed of over 70 miles per hour.
SATURDAY *May 6*	The Kentucky Derby is won by a horse named Sunday Silence, ridden by jockey Pat Valenzuela.
SUNDAY *May 7*	8 people get stuck upside-down, 60 feet in the air, for 2 ½ hours on a ride called the Super Loop in Far Rockaway, New York. They are rescued by firefighters.
MONDAY *May 8*	The space shuttle *Atlantis,* carrying 5 astronauts, returns to earth at Edwards Air Force Base in California as a crowd of 30,000 people cheers.

WHO ELSE WAS BORN IN MAY?
NELLIE BLY (Elizabeth Cochrane)

U.S. reporter

In 1889, she traveled around the world in 72 days, 6 hours, and 11 minutes, breaking the imaginary record set in the novel *Around the World in Eighty Days*. She was the first woman to make such a trip by herself. She also pretended she was insane in order to get a story about the poor conditions in Blackwell's Island Asylum.

BORN   May 5, 1867, in Cochran's Mills, Pennsylvania

TUESDAY
May 9
A Picasso self-portrait sells for $47,800,000 in New York City, the highest price ever for a 20th-century painting.

WEDNESDAY
May 10
The first Japanese high school in the U.S. opens today in Sweetwater, Tennessee. It's called Tennessee Meiji Gakuin and is for Japanese children who are living temporarily in the U.S.

THURSDAY
May 11
The Pentagon's first test of a Midgetman missile fails. It begins to tumble 70 seconds after lift-off and is blown up over the Pacific Ocean.

FRIDAY
May 12
David Lambert catches a record-breaking 24-pound, 3-ounce whiterock bass at Leesville Lake in Virginia.

SATURDAY
May 13
About 150 children come to Norfolk, Virginia, to attend a reunion for test-tube babies. The world's first test-tube baby is Louise Brown, who was born in Great Britain on July 25, 1978.

SUNDAY
May 14
Mother's Day • Robert Swan becomes the first person to walk to both ends of the earth when he and his icewalk team reach the North Pole after a 55-day trek.

MONDAY
May 15
TWISTERS GALORE: 2 tornadoes whip through Texas, 2 touch down in Oklahoma, 2 hit Florida, and 1 strikes New Mexico!
• 27,000 teachers go on strike in Los Angeles, California.

TUESDAY
May 16
The city of Nashville, Tennessee, votes *not* to build a launching pad for UFOs to land on. A disappointed councilman says the people of Nashville will be sorry later.

WEDNESDAY
May 17

A California condor chick begins poking through its eggshell at the San Diego Zoo. It's the 3d condor conceived in captivity.
• In Cleburne, Texas, helicopter pilot David Siegel lifts 2 children from the top of a car just before it is swept into a flooded creek.

THURSDAY
May 18

2 Canadian scientists report that the water level of the world's oceans seems to have risen 1/10 of an inch over the past 100 years. This could be a sign that the planet is getting a little warmer every year.

FRIDAY
May 19

15-year-old Jack Staddon of Great Bend, Kansas, wins the National Geography Bee in Washington, D.C. His prize is a $25,000 scholarship.

SATURDAY
May 20
Full Moon

The Preakness Stakes is won by Sunday Silence, the same horse that won the Kentucky Derby on May 6. • International Chicken Flying Meet in Columbus, Ohio.

SUNDAY
May 21

At the Calaveras County Fair and Jumping Frog Jubilee, a frog named Heavy Metal wins with a mighty leap of 19 feet, 9¼ inches. The frog's owner is Tom Beatty of Bend, Oregon.

MONDAY
May 22

GOOFY GEESE: In Cincinnati, 2 Canada geese have put 12 golf balls in their nest along with 3 of their eggs. Officials think the geese have mistaken the balls for eggs.

TUESDAY
May 23

Stefania Follini breaks the women's world record for living underground when she emerges from a cave in New Mexico, where she has lived for 130 days.

CAVE WOMAN

As part of a scientific experiment to see how people are affected by being alone for a long time, a 27-year-old woman named Stefania Follini spends 130 days by herself in an underground cave near Carlsbad, New Mexico. She enters the cave on January 13th. To pass the time, she plays her guitar, reads, exercises, and makes friends with the mice, frogs, and grasshoppers in the cave.

What are the results of the experiment? By the time she surfaces on May 23, she can concentrate better, but she has lost track of time. She thinks it's March!

Hello, Mr. Mouse!

WEDNESDAY
May 24

The movie *Indiana Jones and the Last Crusade* opens today.
• U.S. wildlife officials announce that at least 42 eagles have died from the Exxon oil tanker spill in Alaska.

THURSDAY
May 25

The National Hockey League's Stanley Cup is won by the Calgary Flames. • Mikhail Gorbachev is reelected president of the Soviet Union by the new Soviet parliament.

FRIDAY
May 26

A new record is set when a boat called the *Great American* sails under the Golden Gate Bridge. It has made a 14,500-mile trip from New York City to San Francisco in just 76 days, 23 hours.

SATURDAY
May 27

A group of international astronomers discover an exploded star in the constellation Cygnus. They think the star is becoming a black hole.

SUNDAY
May 28

The Indianapolis 500 automobile race is won by Emerson Fittipaldi of Brazil, with an average speed of 167.581. • Ed Passerini wins the American *Tour de Sol,* a 210-mile race for solar powered cars that began May 25.

MONDAY
May 29

Memorial Day • A rare right whale and her baby are spotted 1/4 mile off Stone Harbor, New Jersey. There are only about 170 left in the world.

TUESDAY
May 30

Andy Warhol's painting *Shot Red Marilyn* is sold in New York City for $4,070,000—the highest price ever paid for one of his paintings.

WEDNESDAY
May 31

Lava erupts from the volcano Kilauea in Hawaii for the first time in a year.

FAMILY WINS LIFETIME FREE PASSES TO ALL DISNEY ATTRACTIONS

A McDONALD'S FOR HORSES OPENS IN FLORIDA

UNDERWATER GEYSERS ARE ERUPTING ON FLOOR OF MEDITERRANEAN SEA

100,000 PEOPLE PROTEST FOR DEMOCRACY IN BEIJING

June

June is named for the Latin *juniores,* meaning "youths," or from the goddess Juno.

BIRTHSTONE *Pearl*

THURSDAY
June 1

In Washington, D.C., 14-year-old Scott Isaacs of Littleton, Colorado, wins the Scripps-Howard National Spelling Bee. Winning word: spoliator (a spoiler). He practiced for the bee by studying 104 words a day for 6 months.

FRIDAY
June 2

The oil slick in Alaskan waters is now the size of Vermont. At least 33,000 birds, 980 otters, 32 seals, 19 whales, 14 sea lions, and 6 porpoises have died.

SATURDAY
June 3

A 223-year-old secretary (a combination desk and bookcase) is sold for $12,100,000 in New York City. This is a record price for a piece of furniture.

SUNDAY
June 4

A train jumps the tracks near Torrance, Pennsylvania, spilling thousands of gallons of corn syrup. • Balvinder Singh wins the Vertical Marathon by climbing the 1,336 stairs of the world's tallest hotel—the Westin Stamford Hotel in Singapore—in 6 minutes, 55 seconds.

MONDAY
June 5

11-year-old Tony Aliengena, the youngest pilot to fly across the U.S., takes off from Costa Mesa, California, to try to become the youngest person to fly around the world.

TUESDAY
June 6

People of Sacramento, California, vote to shut down the Rancho Seco nuclear power plant. This is the first closing of a nuclear power plant by popular vote.

WEDNESDAY
June 7

Ron Johnson and Rene Coker, who are both clowns with the Ringling Bros. and Barnum & Bailey Circus, are married today just before the afternoon show. After the wedding they ride off on an elephant wearing a JUST MARRIED sign.

THURSDAY
June 8

Rudy Vega returns a bag of money that fell off an armored truck yesterday in El Paso, Texas. There is $440,000 inside the bag.

WHO ELSE WAS BORN IN JUNE?
GERONIMO

Apache Indian chief
Many people consider Geronimo the greatest war leader of the Apache Indians. After his Arizona tribe was forced to move to a reservation, he led many raids in Mexico and the U.S. His Native American name, *Goyathlay*, means "One Who Yawns."
BORN   June 16, 1829, in Arizona

FRIDAY
June 9

The movie *Star Trek V: The Final Frontier* opens today. • Half of this year's crop of 47,000,000 California oranges are only the size of tennis balls, due to a drought in the spring.

SATURDAY
June 10

The Belmont Stakes is won by a horse named Easy Goer, ridden by jockey Pat Day.

SUNDAY
June 11

SSSSTOWAWAY: A 4-foot-long snake is seen slithering down the aisle of a plane about to take off from Baltimore, Maryland. It turns out to be a harmless gopher snake and is taken to a pet store.

MONDAY
June 12

The Elvis Presley Automobile Museum opens in Memphis, Tennessee. It houses 20 cars that used to belong to the famous singer, including a pink Cadillac he bought for his mother.

TUESDAY
June 13

The Detroit Pistons win the NBA basketball championship, beating the Los Angeles Lakers 4 games to 0.

WEDNESDAY
June 14

Two koalas, Billi and Miji from the San Diego Zoo in California, arrive at the London Zoo, along with a large bunch of eucalyptus leaves. Fresh supplies will be flown across the Atlantic twice a week to keep them happy.

THURSDAY
June 15

A meteorite crashes to earth on North Island in New Zealand.
• A window washer in Phoenix, Arizona, is rescued after a rope slips and he hangs 20 stories above the street for 2 hours.

THE EIFFEL TOWER

The Eiffel Tower in Paris is the most famous building in France. It was commissioned by the French government to celebrate the 100th anniversary of the French Revolution, which took place in 1789. Designed by Gustave Eiffel, it took 18 months to build and was completed on March 31, 1889. It is made completely of iron and weighs 8,090 tons.

The world's tallest building for 40 years, the Eiffel Tower is 985 feet, 11 inches tall. There are 1,792 steps to the top. In June of 1989, a huge party—with 800,000 guests—is held to celebrate the building's 100th birthday. More than 5,000,000 people visit the Eiffel Tower this year.

FRIDAY
June 16

A new record is set when 4 golfers shoot holes-in-one in the second round of the U.S. Open in Pittsford, New York. • A pecan pie weighing 40,266 pounds, with a diameter of 40 feet, is baked in Okmulgee, Oklahoma. It's the largest and heaviest pie ever made.

SATURDAY
June 17

The Eiffel Tower in Paris celebrates its 100th birthday with fireworks and a 65-foot-wide birthday cake. • A male Sichuan takin calf is born at the San Diego Zoo in California. It is the first of this species to be born outside of China.

SUNDAY
June 18

Father's Day • 11-year-old Tony Aliengena flies his plane from Iceland to Norway. He is trying to become the youngest pilot to fly around the world.

MONDAY
June 19

Full Moon

Wildfires are out of control in the Florida Everglades. 40,000 acres have burned.

TUESDAY
June 20

Thousands of toadfish arrive in Sausalito, California, keeping the people who live there awake with their loud humming. A toadfish hums to attract a mate.

WEDNESDAY
June 21

Summer solstice • Happy birthday to Prince William of England; he is 7 today. • A company in Sunnyvale, California, has invented a wheelchair that can climb stairs.

FUN FACT '89

You can blink an eyelash for about 150 days before it falls out.

THURSDAY *June 22*	Scientists explode a powerful nuclear weapon 6,800 feet below the surface of the Nevada desert.
FRIDAY *June 23*	The film *Batman* opens in 2,850 movie theaters across the U.S. So many people rush to see it that it makes $13,100,000 in one day, breaking all box office records.
SATURDAY *June 24*	In Luling, Texas, Lee Wheelis sets a new record for spitting a watermelon seed. The seed travels 68 feet, 9⅛ inches.
SUNDAY *June 25*	An earthquake caused by the eruption of Kilauea volcano shakes Hawaii Island, creating a small tidal wave. The earthquake measures 6.1 on the Richter scale.
MONDAY *June 26*	A Spanish galleon that sank sometime in the early 1600s has been found 1,500 feet below the surface of the ocean near southwest Florida. • Tony Aliengena lands in Moscow on his way to becoming the youngest pilot to fly around the world.
TUESDAY *June 27*	Fisherman Mike Shannon lands a 2-pound, 10-ounce Apache trout in the Apache Reservoir in Arizona, a record size for this kind of fish.
WEDNESDAY *June 28*	9 mountain climbers from Australia scale the 22,205-foot-high Mt. Huascarán in Peru, carrying a dining table and chairs. When they get to the top, they dress up in tuxedos and ball dresses and eat a three-course meal!
THURSDAY *June 29*	A 46-year-old man is arrested in Elroy, Texas, for poisoning a 500-year-old tree in Austin called the Treaty Oak. He used a deadly herbicide called Velpar.
FRIDAY *June 30*	At the International Rope Skipping Competition in Greeley, Colorado, 200 people jump the same rope together, breaking the world record for most people on one rope.

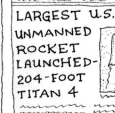

One man stops whole convoy of tanks in China

LARGEST U.S. UNMANNED ROCKET LAUNCHED— 204-FOOT TITAN 4

Sitting Bull's shirt sold to dentist in South Dakota

7-YEAR-OLD TEXAS GIRL SURVIVES 15 HOURS IN SEWER

July

This month was named to honor Julius Caesar.

BIRTHSTONE *Ruby*

SATURDAY
July 1

July is National Anti-Boredom Month • Eau Claire, Michigan: The International Cherry Pit Spitting Contest is won for the 7th time by an elementary school teacher, Rick "Pellet Gun" Krause. He spits his pit 59 feet, 6 inches.

SUNDAY
July 2

People are flocking to see the brand new exhibit at the San Diego Zoo in California: Sun Bear Forest. Sun bears are the smallest of bears; they are only 3 to 4 feet long.

MONDAY
July 3

Workers in Austin, Texas, begin putting up 65-foot-tall sunscreens around the Treaty Oak to try to keep it from dying. The 500-year-old tree was poisoned last month.

TUESDAY
July 4

Independence Day • Former President Ronald Reagan falls off a horse in Mexico. His injuries are minor.

WEDNESDAY
July 5

Air travel is restricted over parts of Utah and Colorado today because of forest fires, which are burning out of control. The wind is whipping up the fires and sending smoke 10,000 feet in the air.

DINOSAUR DISCOVERY

In 1989 the oldest known dinosaur is found at the foot of the Andes Mountains in Argentina. Scientists unearth an almost complete skeleton of an 8-foot-tall *Herrerasaurus*, which lived about 230,000,000 years ago. The dinosaur is named after fossil hunter Victorino Herrera, who discovered small pieces of its bones many years ago. The *Herrerasaurus* walked on its hind legs, had a dual-hinged jaw, was a meat-eater, and weighed about 300 pounds.

WHO ELSE WAS BORN IN JULY?
SAMUEL DE CHAMPLAIN

French explorer; first governor of French Canada
After voyages to the Canary Islands and Central
America, he explored Nova Scotia and made maps
of the coast of New England. In 1608—on his
41st birthday—he founded Quebec in Canada. He
discovered Lake Champlain in 1609.
BORN July 3, 1567, in Brouage, France

THURSDAY
July 6

The New York Aquarium Discovery Cove opens in Brooklyn,
with mechanically generated surf to show how beaches are
formed. Visitors can also experience firsthand the crash of a
wave dumping 400 gallons of water into a tidal pool.

FRIDAY
July 7

NASA announces that space probe *Voyager 2* has discovered a
3d moon orbiting the planet Neptune. • A U.S. silver dollar
from 1804 is sold for $990,000 in Chicago, Illinois, the
highest price ever paid for a single coin.

SATURDAY
July 8

Happy 31st birthday to Willie B., a gorilla at the zoo in
Atlanta, Georgia. He is given a party and a special treat: a
banana split!

SUNDAY
July 9

Boris Becker of West Germany wins the men's singles tennis
title at Wimbledon in England. Steffi Graf of West Germany
wins the women's singles.

MONDAY
July 10

Tornadoes destroy more than 100 homes in Massachusetts,
New York, New Jersey, and Connecticut. • There are 31,000
fires burning out of control in 10 states, caused by dry weather
and lightning.

TUESDAY
July 11

In Phoenix, Arizona, U.S. Secret Service agents seize
$1,000,000 in counterfeit money. They suspect the $100 bills
were made by using a photocopy machine. • The American
League wins baseball's All-Star game, 5–3.

FUN FACT '89

In 1989 the richest man in the U.S. is Sam Moore Walton, who is
reported to have $8.7 billion.

WEDNESDAY
July 12

A firefighter named Fritz Elk, who is also a Sioux Indian, does a rain dance in Boulder Canyon, Colorado. 30 minutes later, it begins to rain! The rain helps to douse the raging wildfires. 1,500,000 acres have been scorched in 6 western states.

THURSDAY
July 13

BRIDGE BUZZING: A single-engine airplane zooms over and under 5 Willamette River bridges in Portland, Oregon. The plane comes within only 20 feet of hitting a tugboat.

FRIDAY
July 14

Bastille Day. To mark the 200th anniversary of the French Revolution, the U.S. Postal Service issues a special 45-cent airmail stamp. France celebrates with a huge parade, including 5,200 soldiers and 300 tanks, accompanied by 250 planes and helicopters.

SATURDAY
July 15

At the annual meeting of the Jim Smith Society in Bethesda, Maryland, about 60 people named Jim Smith from 16 states play softball together.

SUNDAY
July 16

National Ice Cream Day • 10 rare black rhinoceroses from Africa arrive by jumbo jet in Grapevine, Texas. They are headed for various U.S. zoos and ranches to be bred in the hope of saving the species.

WHAT'S HOT IN 1989

Hypercars	Barbie
Talking baseball cards	Food Fighters (action figures)
Game Boy	CD players
"Tetris"	Electronic diaries
Mountain bikes	Pieces of the Berlin Wall

Batman anything: Batman action figures, Batman trading cards, Batmobiles, Batcaves, Batpins, Batbuttons, Batshoes, Bat T-shirts, Batwatches, Batsweatshirts, Bat-pj's, Batsheets, Bathats, Batsuspenders, even Bat-boxer shorts.

Hot haircuts: Hair etching and the Flip

MONDAY
July 17

The radar-avoiding B2 Stealth bomber makes its first flight over the Mojave Desert in California. It looks like a huge boomerang.

TUESDAY
July 18
Full Moon

In Nairobi, the president of Kenya sets a pile of 12 tons of elephant tusks on fire. He is trying to make people stop killing the endangered elephants for their tusks.

WEDNESDAY
July 19

A new elephant house opens at the Bronx Zoo in New York. It's much more realistic than the old one and contains Malayan tapirs and Indian rhinoceroses as well as elephants.

THURSDAY
July 20

Today is the 20th anniversary of the first landing on the moon. To commemorate the occasion, the U.S. Postal Service issues a new stamp that pictures 2 astronauts placing an American flag on the moon.

FRIDAY
July 21

300 people on bicycles arrive in Atlantic City, New Jersey, after pedaling 3,359 miles from Seattle, Washington, in the 47-day TransAmerica Bicycle Trek. The leader is Gerald Wright, who has a cast on his leg!

SATURDAY
July 22

In Baltimore, Maryland, 524 jugglers juggle 1,997 objects in the air at the same time, setting the world record for most jugglers juggling the greatest number of objects at once.

SUNDAY
July 23

Greg LeMond of the U.S. wins the 2,030 mile Tour de France bicycle race by only 8 seconds! It's the closest race in Tour de France history.
• The longest sand sculpture in the world is made in Long Beach, Washington. It's 15,734 feet long.

MONDAY
July 24

The U.S. Fish and Wildlife Service declares the desert tortoise an endangered species.

TUESDAY
July 25

Sean Shannon of Oxford, England, becomes the world's fastest talker after reciting a 260-word speech in 26.8 seconds.
• The governor of New York makes the ladybug (*Coccinella novemnotata*) the official state insect.

WEDNESDAY *July 26*	Mark Wellman becomes the first paraplegic (a person paralyzed from the waist down) to climb 3,600 feet to the top of El Capitan, a mountain in California. • The tallest sand sculpture in the world is built in Japan by 2,000 volunteers. It is 56 feet, 2 inches high.
THURSDAY *July 27*	18 Kemps Ridley sea turtles are hatched in Madeira Beach, Florida. It's the first recorded hatching of the world's rarest turtles.
FRIDAY *July 28*	Sonny Manley catches a record-breaking Atlantic halibut off Gloucester, Massachusetts. The fish weighs 255 pounds, 4 ounces!
SATURDAY *July 29*	Cuban athlete Javier Sotomayor breaks the high-jump record at the Caribbean championships in Puerto Rico, clearing the 8-foot barrier.
SUNDAY *July 30*	The National Scrabble Championship begins in New York City. 230 people enter; they each must play 27 games. • UFOs reported over London.
MONDAY *July 31*	9-year-old Ian Hawthorne, who was lost overnight on a cold mountainside in Deckers, Colorado, is rescued by a KUSA-TV helicopter from Denver.

TONY ALIENGENA, 11, BECOMES YOUNGEST PILOT TO FLY AROUND WORLD

BANK ROBBER MUGGED AFTER PULLING JOB IN BROOKLYN

Antinuclear protestors force Navy to cancel missle test

First free elections in Poland since World War II

August

August was named in honor of Roman emperor
Augustus, whose lucky month it was.

BIRTHSTONE *Peridot*

TUESDAY
August 1

6 explorers begin a 4,000-mile trek across Antarctica on skis, with 42 dogs pulling supplies on sleds. They have face cream and special clothes to block out the sun's harmful rays. They are attempting to be the first people to cross Antarctica without any motorized vehicles.

WEDNESDAY
August 2

A Boeing 737 jet makes an emergency landing in Greensboro, North Carolina, after its landing gear fails to open.

THURSDAY
August 3

The U.S. Forest Service reports that more than 39,400 fires have burned 1,380,000 acres in the western U.S. Major fires are still raging in Idaho, Oregon, California, and Montana.

FRIDAY
August 4

30,000 Boy Scouts from around the world are having fun at the Boy Scout Jamboree at Fort A.P. Hill, Virginia. By the end of the 4-day celebration, they have drunk 25,000 packages of cocoa and eaten 17.5 tons of hamburger.

SATURDAY
August 5

THE REAL WHOPPER: The world's biggest hamburger is made in Seymour, Wisconsin. It weighs 5,520 pounds!
• In Twinsburg, Ohio, about 2,500 sets of twins attend the annual Twins Day Festival.

SUNDAY
August 6

32-year-old American Kate Goodale becomes the 364th person to swim across the English Channel, in 11 hours, 53 minutes.

MONDAY
August 7

National Lighthouse Day. It's the 200th anniversary of U.S. lighthouses.

TUESDAY
August 8

U.S. space shuttle *Columbia* blasts off, carrying 2 secret military satellites. • An *Ariane 4* rocket is also launched, from French Guiana, to put an astronomy satellite into orbit.

WEDNESDAY *August 9*	Toshiki Kaifu becomes the premier of Japan. • Mild earthquakes rumble in south central Utah and in the San Bernadino National Forest in California.
THURSDAY *August 10*	Scientists in Norway have discovered that there are 1.25 billion viruses in a teaspoon of unpolluted water. They think the viruses kill bacteria.
FRIDAY *August 11*	Space probe *Voyager 2,* which is on its way to Neptune, sends back pictures of 2 partial rings around the planet. *Voyager 2* is 2.8 billion miles from Earth.
SATURDAY *August 12*	The world's largest salami is displayed at the Lebanon Bologna Festival in Kutztown, Pennsylvania. It's 61 feet, 3½ inches long. • Perseid meteor showers tonight!
SUNDAY *August 13*	*Columbia* lands at Edwards Air Force Base in California after a 5-day mission. • A record number of tap dancers—4,877—participate in the annual Tap-o-mania, held in front of Macy's department store in New York City.

LITTLE LEAGUE TURNS 50

The first Little League baseball game was played on June 6, 1939, in Williamsport, Pennsylvania, when "Lundy Lumber" beat "Lycoming Dairy" 23–8. The 20 ballplayers wore uniforms that cost $1.58 each. Today there are 2,500,000 players, between the ages of 6 and 18, on 140,000 teams in 34 nations throughout the world. There is even a Little League museum in Baxter Springs, Kansas, where visitors can see the gloves worn by Mickey Mantle, Yogi Berra, and other famous players.

In August of 1989, an American team wins the Little League World Series for the first time since 1983. Trumbull, Connecticut, beats Kaohsiung, Taiwan 5–2.

WHO ELSE WAS BORN IN AUGUST?
COUNT BASIE (born WILLIAM BASIE)

U.S. jazz musician
Count Basie was a pianist, composer, and bandleader. His "big band" included some of the best jazz musicians of the 1930s and 1940s, and was featured in many motion pictures. He performed with his band right up until his death in 1984, even though by then he was in a wheelchair.
BORN   August 21, 1904, in Red Bank, New Jersey

MONDAY
August 14

A 150-pound black bear falls to the ground from a 25-foot-high utility pole in Albuquerque, New Mexico. Officials couldn't get her down so they shot her with a tranquilizer gun.

TUESDAY
August 15

PLAY *MIACH*! The Soviet Union's first baseball park is unveiled today.

WEDNESDAY
August 16

Full Moon

A total eclipse of the moon occurs at 9:21 P.M. (EDT). It can be seen in the northeastern U.S. and in parts of South America, Africa, Europe, and Greenland.

THURSDAY
August 17

A 20-foot-long, 250-pound reticulated python is captured under a house in Fort Lauderdale, Florida.

FRIDAY
August 18

COPTER CAPER: 2 women free their husbands from an Arkansas state prison by hijacking a helicopter to pluck them out of the prison yard. They are all caught and arrested. • 79 women make a free-fall parachute jump together in Montgomery, New York.

SATURDAY
August 19

Multimillionaire Malcolm Forbes throws a party at his palace in Morocco to celebrate his 70th birthday. The 600 guests are greeted by 3 camels and thousands of balloons. The entertainment includes fireworks, drummers, and 600 belly dancers, acrobats, and jugglers!

CLOSE ENCOUNTER WITH NEPTUNE

When U.S. space probe *Voyager 2* comes within 3,000 miles of the cloudtops of the planet Neptune, it is moving at a speed of 38,000 miles an hour and is 2.8 billion miles away from Earth.

Voyager 2 sends back photographs that show that Neptune has 4 rings around it and at least 8 moons. The largest moon, Triton, is a pretty pink color and is covered with ice volcanoes. Triton is the coldest place in the entire solar system—400°F below 0!

Voyager 2 has been traveling in space for 12 years. It has already been to Jupiter, Saturn and, Uranus.

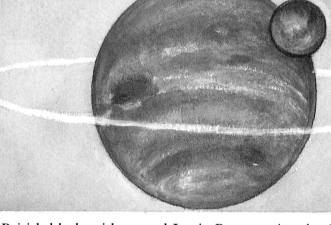

SUNDAY *August 20*	A British blacksmith named Jamie Reeves wins the Strongest Man in the World title in San Sebastian, Spain. • A sacred pole topped with a human scalp is returned to the Omaha Indians after being in a museum in Massachusetts for 101 years.
MONDAY *August 21*	*Voyager 2,* now only 3,000,000 miles from Neptune, sends back to earth photographs of one of Neptune's moons, Triton. It's pink, with blue around the equator.
TUESDAY *August 22*	Nolan Ryan of the Texas Rangers becomes the first baseball pitcher to strike out 5,000 batters. He strikes out his 5,000th—Ricky Henderson—in a game against the Oakland Athletics.
WEDNESDAY *August 23*	13-year-old Victoria Brucker becomes the first girl to play—and pitch—in the U.S. Little League Championship playoffs in Williamsport, Pennsylvania. Unfortunately, her San Pedro, California, team loses to the team from Trumbull, Connecticut.

FUN FACT '89

Antarctica is bigger than all of China and India put together.

THURSDAY
August 24

After a 12-year flight from Earth, during which it traveled 4.4 billion miles, *Voyager 2* space probe is only one second late when it passes close by Neptune today at 11:56 P.M. (EDT).

FRIDAY
August 25

In areas throughout New England, the mosquitoes are biting at a rate of 30 bites a minute!

SATURDAY
August 26

As a crowd of 40,000 watches, the baseball team from Trumbull, Connecticut, beats the Taiwan team 5–2 in the Little League World Series in Williamsport, Pennsylvania.

SUNDAY
August 27

Mission Control throws a huge party to celebrate *Voyager 2*'s flight to Neptune. • 1.25 tons of silver has been stolen from a mine near Lovelock, Nevada. The silver is in the form of small pieces that look like Chocolate Kisses.

MONDAY
August 28

Astronomers in the U.S. and Puerto Rico have discovered what they think is a galaxy being born, about 65,000,000 light-years from earth.

TUESDAY
August 29

More than 2,900 teachers go on strike in Illinois, Pennsylvania, Ohio, Michigan, and Montana.

WEDNESDAY
August 30

At Cape Canaveral in Florida, the *Galileo* space probe is loaded into space shuttle *Atlantis* to prepare for its launch in October. *Galileo* is being sent to Jupiter!

THURSDAY
August 31

A partial eclipse of the sun can be seen in southeastern Africa, Madagascar, and parts of Antarctica. • 100 years ago today the pay phone was patented.

PETE ROSE BANNED FOREVER FROM BASEBALL FOR BETTING ON GAMES

SPACE SHUTTLE SONIC BOOM MAKES BUILDINGS SWAY IN LOS ANGELES

COUPLE RESCUED AFTER 66 DAYS OF DRIFTING IN RUBBER BOAT

Ice cream trucks told to keep music low in Boulder, Colorado

September

*T*he name September comes from the latin *septem,* meaning "seven." This was the seventh month of the old Roman calendar.

BIRTHSTONE *Sapphire*

FRIDAY
September 1

Giant panda Ling-Ling gives birth to a 4-ounce baby panda at the National Zoo in Washington. • The Nevado del Ruiz volcano in Colombia spouts steam and ash. 2,300 people are evacuated.

SATURDAY
September 2

The largest bottle in the world is displayed in Queensland in Australia. It is 6 feet, 11 inches tall and 5 feet, 4½ inches around.

SUNDAY
September 3

A sick, 900-pound baby sperm whale washes up on a beach in Galveston, Texas.

MONDAY
September 4

Labor Day • In Compton, California, a car carrying 14 people plunges 70 feet down into a quarry. Miraculously, the car lands on all four wheels, and no one is hurt!

TUESDAY
September 5

Soviet cosmonauts Aleksander Serebrov and Aleksander Viktorenko blast off in a *Soyuz TM8* spacecraft to join the orbiting space station *Mir* for 6 months.

WEDNESDAY
September 6

Ileana Ros-Lehtinen of Miami, Florida, is sworn in, becoming the first Cuban American in the U.S. Congress. She left Cuba and came to the United States when she was 7.

THURSDAY
September 7

Hurricane Gabrielle's 105-mile-per-hour winds hit the coast of Bermuda, causing 20-foot-high waves.

FRIDAY
September 8

The 2 cosmonauts who left earth Wednesday make a manual linkup with space station *Mir* after the automatic docking system fails.

SATURDAY
September 9

Workers in the mangrove forests in India have started wearing masks on the back of their heads to keep Bengal tigers from attacking. The tigers only attack from behind. So far the masks seem to be fooling the tigers; no one wearing a mask has been attacked.

WHO ELSE WAS BORN IN SEPTEMBER?
JIM ABBOT

U.S. baseball player
Winner of the Sullivan Award in the 1988
Olympics. He began his major-league pitching
career with the California Angels in 1988. He was
born without a right hand.
BORN   September 19, 1967, in Flint, Michigan

SUNDAY
September 10

Grandparents' Day • U.S. officials have ordered shrimp fishermen to install trapdoor devices in their nets to protect endangered sea turtles from getting caught.

MONDAY
September 11

A new lake is created when 25,000 cubic yards of rock falls into a gorge near Grants Pass, Oregon. The new lake is 2,000 feet long and 50 feet deep.

TUESDAY
September 12

1,000,000 rubber tires are on fire in a dump in Danville, New Hampshire. The smoke can be seen for 25 miles. The fire is so hot that firefighters have to use dirt to try to put it out—water just turns into steam!

WEDNESDAY
September 13

BEE CAREFUL: Large swarms of meat-eating bees are stinging people along the West Coast of the U.S. They are called meat bees and are meaner than the average bee.

THURSDAY
September 14

Treasure hunters begin raising gold bars and coins from the wreck of the steamer SS *Central America,* which sank off the coast of South Carolina in 1857 with about 3 tons of gold on board.

FRIDAY
September 15

Full Moon

Ashrita Furman sets a new distance record for pogo stick jumping, 13.06 miles, in New York City. It takes him 5 hours and 23 minutes.

SATURDAY
September 16

Oxford University beats Cambridge University in the annual Oxford-Cambridge boat race. Usually it is held on the Thames River in England, but this year it is held on the Chicago River in Illinois.

WHAT'S NEW IN 1989

Frosty Paws an ice-creamlike treat for dogs

Filmless photography images stored on a computer disk

Craisins sugared, dried cranberries the size of raisins

Rabbi trading cards collectible cards featuring famous rabbis

A glass submarine for tourists in Hawaii to explore underwater

Soviet baseball the first baseball park in Russia opens

The Pet Chime a doorbell for dogs or cats

Crop circles mysterious circles that appear in British fields

Symphony a new milk-chocolate bar from Hershey

HDTV high definition television

Power Pad video game controlled by jumping on a vinyl mat

SUNDAY
September 17

Hurricane Hugo hits the Virgin Islands with 96-mile-per-hour winds. Tin roofs are ripped off buildings; many people are without homes.

MONDAY
September 18

Hurricane Hugo slams into Puerto Rico, knocking out most of the electricity. The water is waist deep in some areas of the city of San Juan. 300,000 people have already been evacuated.

TUESDAY
September 19

A brown teddy bear made by Steiff of Germany is sold for 55,100 pounds (about $88,160) in London, England. It's the most ever paid for a teddy bear!

WEDNESDAY
September 20

In France, the new high-speed train, the *TGV Atlantique*, makes its first trip from Paris to Le Mans. It runs at 186 miles per hour today, but can reach a speed of 233 miles per hour.

THURSDAY
September 21

Hugo, the most powerful hurricane to hit the U.S. in 20 years, reaches Charleston, South Carolina. Many buildings are completely flattened, and the roof is blown off City Hall.

FRIDAY
September 22

Autumn equinox • Hurricane Hugo hits Charlotte, North Carolina, with winds of up to 135 miles per hour before heading inland.

SATURDAY
September 23

TRASH BASH: 64,500 volunteers in Florida collect garbage along 2,900 miles of shoreline as part of the "National Beach Clean-Up Campaign." One of the volunteers finds a live octopus inside a beer bottle.

FUN FACT '89

By the time a person in the U.S. is 18 years old, he or she has spent 2 whole years watching TV.

SUNDAY
September 24

Temperatures drop below 32°F in southern Missouri. It's the earliest freeze ever for this part of the U.S.

MONDAY
September 25

About 435,000 students in Utah have a holiday from school today. All the teachers in the state are on strike. Teachers in 5 other states are also striking.

TUESDAY
September 26

Hershey launches a new chocolate bar today called Symphony. It's the first new milk-chocolate bar from Hershey in almost 100 years.

WEDNESDAY
September 27

Peter DeBernardi and Jeffrey Petkovich ride over Niagara Falls together in a barrel.
• In Bellingham, Washington, a pet bull named Fernando wanders out of his pasture and traps 5 people in a store for 45 minutes.

THURSDAY
September 28

11-year-old Paul Smith of Larain, Ohio, is honored at the White House today for pulling a younger child out of the way of an oncoming car. Paul was on school safety patrol duty at the time.

FRIDAY
September 29

Rosh Hashanah begins at sundown. • WORLD'S BIGGEST BUST: Law officers in Los Angeles seize 22 tons of cocaine and $10,000,000 in cash.

SATURDAY
September 30

Thousands of Byelorussians march through the center of Minsk in the Soviet Union to try to force the government to do more to clean up after the 1986 nuclear power plant accident at Chernobyl.

BARBIE BREAKFAST CEREAL ARRIVES AT SUPERMARKETS

Underground thermal explosion destroys geyser at Yellowstone National Park

ROOF FALLS INTO SWIMMING POOL AT BOSTON YMCA

10-YEAR-OLD FOUND IN UTAH MINE AFTER BEING LOST 5 DAYS

2 + 2 = 4

October

*O*ctober was the eighth month of the old Roman calendar; the name is from the Latin *octo,* meaning "eight."

BIRTHSTONE *Opal*

SUNDAY
October 1

DINOSAUR MAIL: A block of four 25-cent dinosaur stamps is issued by the U.S. Postal Service to honor Stamp Collecting Month.

MONDAY
October 2

59 square miles of the Mojave Desert is closed to the public today to try to protect the endangered desert tortoise.

TUESDAY
October 3

5,000,000 pounds of butter melts into a gooey mess when fire breaks out in a warehouse in Cambridge, Maryland. 300 firefighters combat the flames for 21 hours!

WEDNESDAY
October 4

The National Science Foundation announces that the oldest rocks in the world have been found in northern Canada. They are 3,960,000,000 years old. • Coyote alert in Kent, New York.

THURSDAY
October 5

His Holiness Tenzin Gyatso, Dalai Lama of Tibet, is awarded the Nobel Peace Prize for his efforts to liberate his people and for his respect for all living things.

FRIDAY
October 6

HOT CHOCOLATE, ANYONE? 70 tons of chocolate are destroyed in a fire at the Cadbury Chocolate factory in Marlbrook, England.

SATURDAY
October 7

Mount Etna in Italy is erupting, and an airport in Sicily is closed because ash and black dust cover the runways.

SUNDAY
October 8

Yom Kippur begins at sundown • The Oakland Athletics beat the Toronto Blue Jays for the American League Championship in baseball. • Free rides on the carousel today at Middlebury amusement park in Connecticut!

FUN FACT '89

Only 1/3 of the people in the U.S. wash their belly buttons daily.

WHO ELSE WAS BORN IN OCTOBER?
MAHATMA GANDHI (Mohandas Karamchand Gandhi)

Indian political leader and lawyer
Gandhi didn't believe the British government
should rule India. He organized "civil
disobedience" demonstrations which eventually led
to India's independence. He was known for using
only peaceful methods to achieve his goals, and
was a role model for other great leaders, such as
Martin Luther King, Jr.

BORN   October 2, 1869, in Porbandar, India

MONDAY
October 9

The San Francisco Giants beat the Chicago Cubs for
the National League Championship. • Gordon
Thomson of Quebec, Canada, wins the annual
World Pumpkin Confederation contest in Collins,
New York, with his 755-pound pumpkin.

TUESDAY
October 10

The Soviet news agency insists today that its recent
report of a banana-shaped UFO landing in the Russian
city of Voronezh was not a joke. Supposedly, a 9-foot-
tall alien with 3 eyes was seen by a crowd of people.

WEDNESDAY
October 11

A fishing boat sinks in the Pacific near Hawaii. The
6 men who were on board survive by clinging to a raft
made of buoys and nets from the boat.

THURSDAY
October 12

A block of four 24-cent stamps from 1918 featuring an upside-
down airplane is bought for the record high price of
$1,100,000 in New York City. The stamp is called the
"Inverted Jenny."

FRIDAY
October 13

The world's largest chimp exhibit opens at the Detroit Zoo in
Michigan. It covers nearly 4 acres and is the only exhibit in the
U.S. where visitors can interact with chimpanzees. • The 6 men
whose boat sank Wednesday are rescued today, 50 miles off Maui.

SATURDAY
October 14

65,000 people in Wellston, Ohio, are evacuated when a frozen-
pizza factory leaks deadly gas.

Full Moon

TOP TEN SINGLES OF 1989*

1 "Another Day in Paradise"   Phil Collins
2 "Miss You Much"   Janet Jackson
3 "Straight Up"   Paula Abdul
4 "Right Here Waiting"   Richard Marx
5 "Lost in Your Eyes"   Debbie Gibson
6 "Like a Prayer"   Madonna
7 "We Didn't Start the Fire"   Billy Joel
8 "Two Hearts"   Phil Collins
9 "When I See You Smile"   Bad English
10 "Blame It on the Rain"   Milli Vanilli

*Source: *Billboard*

SUNDAY
October 15

National Grouch Day • The first golf course in the Soviet Union opens in Moscow. Several days of rain have made the turf so muddy that the players have to wear boots!

MONDAY
October 16

103 nations vote to ban all trade in ivory to try to save the African elephant from extinction. Ivory hunters are killing the elephants for their tusks.

TUESDAY
October 17

The worst California earthquake since 1906 (6.9 on the Richter scale) strikes San Francisco, destroying a part of the Bay Bridge and a section of a double-decker freeway.

WEDNESDAY
October 18

Space shuttle *Atlantis* is launched from Cape Canaveral, Florida, carrying the spacecraft *Galileo* at the start of its 6-year journey to Jupiter. • The world's largest cake is cut today in Fort Payne, Alabama. It weighs 128,238 pounds, 8 ounces, and was made to celebrate the town's 100th birthday.

THURSDAY
October 19

Three strong aftershocks (2 of them measuring 5 on the Richter scale) hit San Francisco. Five earthquakes also shake northern China.

FRIDAY
October 20

A 1,891.69-gallon milk shake—the largest in the world—is made in Orville, Ohio. It's chocolate.

SATURDAY
October 21

The Wheeling Park High School Marching Band makes it into the *Guinness Book of World Records* when they march and play for almost 15 hours over a distance 42½ miles in Wheeling, West Virginia.

SUNDAY
October 22

World chess champion Gary Kasparov defeats the world champion chess computer in a special 2 game match in New York City. The computer is called Deep Thought.

MONDAY
October 23

U.S. space shuttle *Atlantis* lands safely at Edwards Air Force Base in California with its crew of 3 men and 2 women, after launching *Galileo* toward Venus on the first half of a trip to the planet Jupiter.

TUESDAY
October 24

This is World Rain Forest Week, to remind people that a section of rain forest the size of a football field is being destroyed every second.

WEDNESDAY
October 25

Buildings in San Francisco sway again as more aftershocks follow the major earthquake that struck 8 days ago.

THURSDAY
October 26

A ruby-and-diamond ring weighing 32.08 carats is sold for the record price of $4,620,000 at an auction in New York City.

FRIDAY
October 27

The teddy bear was named after U.S. President Teddy Roosevelt, who was born on this day in 1858. • The World Series, which was postponed by the October 17th earthquake, continues today in San Francisco, California.

SATURDAY
October 28

Baseball's World Series is won by the Oakland Athletics, who defeat the San Francisco Giants 4 games to 0.

SUNDAY
October 29

In Washington, D.C., 6,000 Frisbee lovers take part in the Ultimate Players Association National Championships.

MONDAY
October 30

A company in Japan buys Rockefeller Center in New York City for $864,000,000. • One of the largest frogs ever caught, a rare African giant frog (*conrana goliath*) is officially weighed today. It is 8 pounds, 1 ounce, and was captured in Cameroon in April by Andy Koffman.

TUESDAY
October 31

Halloween • The most complete skeleton of a *Tyrannosaurus rex* ever found has been uncovered in Montana. It has teeth the size of bananas!

OIL SPILL AT ANTARCTIC BASE COULD CONTAMINATE SNOW AND ICE FOR A CENTURY

385,000,000-YEAR-OLD SPIDER FOSSIL FOUND

COMPUTER VIRUSES INFECT UNIVERSITIES AND BUSINESSES THROUGHOUT WORLD

November

*N*ovember was the ninth month of the old Roman calendar. The name comes from the Latin *novem,* meaning "nine."

BIRTHSTONE *Topaz*

WEDNESDAY
November 1

A 48-year-old woman goes to jail in Norcross, Georgia, for having 4 overdue library books— and for not showing up in court to explain why they are overdue.

THURSDAY
November 2

In Baltimore, Maryland, police arrest a man they find walking down the street with 21 live homing pigeons stuffed in his clothes.

FRIDAY
November 3

Miep Gies, a Dutch woman who helped Anne Frank hide from the Nazis during World War II, is given West Germany's highest civilian medal, the Federal Cross of Merit First Class.

SATURDAY
November 4

More than 500,000 people rally for democracy in East Berlin. • On this day in 1922, the tomb of King Tutankhamen was discovered in Egypt.

SUNDAY
November 5

The New York City Marathon is won by Juma Ikangaa of Tanzania (time: 2 hours, 8 minutes, 1 second) and by Ingrid Kristiansen of Norway (time: 2 hours, 25 minutes, 30 seconds). There are a record number of finishers: 24,588.

MONDAY
November 6

An accident near Croton Falls, New York, causes a yogurt delivery truck to spill fruit-flavored yogurt all over a highway. The road is closed for 5 hours due to extreme stickiness.

TUESDAY
November 7

Election Day • L. Douglas Wilder becomes the first black person to be elected governor of a state when he wins the election in Virginia.

WEDNESDAY
November 8

Willem de Kooning's painting *Interchange* is sold for $20,600,000, an auction record for a living artist. • On a trampoline in London, England, Richard Cobbing sets a new world record for number of somersaults in one minute: 75.

FUN FACT '89

There are 3,500 kittens, 2,000 puppies, and 415 babies born every hour in the U.S.

WHO ELSE WAS BORN IN NOVEMBER?
LOUISA MAY ALCOTT

U.S. writer
She wrote books for teenagers and is most famous for her 1868 novel, *Little Women*, which has sold millions of copies. Her other books include *Little Men*, *Eight Cousins*, and *Jo's Boys*.
BORN   November 29, 1832, in Germantown, Pennsylvania

THURSDAY
November 9

East Germany opens its borders for the first time and allows citizens to leave the country freely.

FRIDAY
November 10

DOWN WITH THE BERLIN WALL!
The wall that has divided Berlin for 28 years is torn down today. About 500,000 East Germans enter West Berlin.

SATURDAY
November 11

Archaeologists from the University of Chicago report that they have found an ancient mass grave at Lake Titicaca in Bolivia. The human bones are from an Indian civilization that existed between 300 B.C. and A.D. 1200.

SUNDAY
November 12

At California Polytechnic State University, Greg McNeil makes a successful test of the world's first human-powered helicopter. It was made by students and works by pedaling. Today it lifts 4 inches off the floor for 2 seconds.

MONDAY
November 13

Full Moon

Children's Book Week begins. • Investigators in France say that they have found 13 artworks, worth about $17,000,000, which were stolen from the home of Pablo Picasso's granddaughter. A restaurant owner was hiding them.

TUESDAY
November 14

Mark Davis of the San Diego Padres wins the Cy Young Award for best pitcher in the National League • 100 years ago today, Nellie Bly began her famous 72-day trip around the world.

WEDNESDAY
November 15

The worst tornado of the year strikes Huntsville, Alabama, with winds of up to 250 miles per hour. • Bret Saberhagen of the Kansas City Royals wins the American League's Cy Young Award.

THURSDAY
November 16

In Punxsutawney, Pennsylvania, Dorothy Bartlebaugh and Russell Marshall are married in Aisle 3 of the County Market store, where they first met while shopping in 1988.

FRIDAY
November 17

President Bush signs a law that will increase the minimum wage rate from $3.35 to $4.25 per hour by April 1, 1991.

SATURDAY
November 18

Happy birthday to Carrie C. White in Palatka, Florida, the oldest living person in the world. She is 115 today!

SUNDAY
November 19

U.S. astronomers announce they have detected a source of light coming from the edge of the universe. • In Rome, Italy, a mysterious 2-pound block of green ice falls through the window of a convent. Authorities think it came from a plane, but no one knows why it is green.

MONDAY
November 20

Robin Yount of the Milwaukee Brewers is elected Most Valuable Player in baseball's American League.

TUESDAY
November 21

Kevin Mitchell of the San Francisco Giants is named the National League's Most Valuable Player. • 11 tons of pieces of the Berlin Wall arrive in Chicago, Illinois. They will be sold as souvenirs.

THE BERLIN WALL

At the end of World War II, Berlin, the capital of Germany, was divided between the United States, Great Britain, France, and the Soviet Union. The part controlled by the Soviet Union was called East Berlin and the rest was called West Berlin. During the years after the war, thousands of East Germans moved to West Germany to seek a new life. On August 13, 1961, to keep East German citizens from fleeing into West Berlin, the East German government built a barbed-wire fence all the way around West Berlin. The fence was later replaced by a 6-foot-high concrete wall, topped with barbed wire. Armed guards patrolled the wall, but many people still tried to escape to the West by crossing the wall. In 1970, the height was raised to 9 feet.

In 1989, East Germany finally decides to open its borders. Germans are so happy they dance on top of the wall or chip away at it with hammers. The demolition of the wall leads to the reunification of Germany.

WEDNESDAY
November 22

U.S. space shuttle *Discovery* blasts off from Cape Canaveral, Florida, tonight to put a secret spy satellite into orbit.

THURSDAY
November 23

Thanksgiving Day • The crew on the space shuttle has a vacuum-packed Thanksgiving dinner of diced turkey with gravy, broccoli au gratin, potato patties, cranberrry sauce, and pumpkin muffins. They can't have pumpkin pie because vibrations during liftoff could turn it into liquid.

FRIDAY
November 24

Margaret Thatcher, the Prime Minister of Great Britain, visits President Bush at Camp David in Maryland.

SATURDAY
November 25

5 people who came to the Blue Mountains of southeastern Washington for sledding fun lose their way today and are reported missing.

SUNDAY
November 26

Happy first birthday to Baby Shamu, the first killer whale born in Texas. The 1,100-pound whale puts out the candle on her birthday cake with a squirt of water.

MONDAY
November 27

The first successful U.S. liver transplant using a live donor takes place in Chicago, Illinois. A mother gives ⅓ of her own liver to her 21-month-old daughter. • The sledders lost since Saturday are found by a pilot who sees a distress signal stamped in the snow.

TUESDAY
November 28

A 30-foot-long city made out of Legos is on display in Washington, D.C. It was built by an architect named Duke Guzey and has houses, shops, trains, boats, and a monorail.

WEDNESDAY
November 29

Rajiv Gandhi resigns as prime minister of India. He was getting more and more unpopular, and people had been accusing his government of being dishonest.

THURSDAY
November 30

2 sinkholes open up in North Arlington, New Jersey. The biggest one is 15 feet wide and 25 feet deep. The sinkholes are caused by underground tunnels left over from a copper mine from the 1700s.

ROMANIAN GYMNAST DEFECTS TO U.S.

WOMAN ARRESTED FOR RAISING PET CHICKENS WITHOUT A PERMIT

THE LITTLE MERMAID OPENS IN U.S. MOVIE THEATERS

December

December used to be the tenth month of the year (the Latin *decem* means "ten"). The old Roman calendar began with March.

BIRTHSTONE *Turquoise*

FRIDAY
December 1

Gymnast Nadia Comaneci arrives in New York City after a daring escape from Romania last week. She wants to be a U.S. citizen.

SATURDAY
December 2

Solar Max, a 5,000-pound satellite, which has been studying the sun for 9 years, falls out of orbit over the Indian Ocean and burns up as it reenters earth's atmosphere.

SUNDAY
December 3

A 26-year-old woman in Pittsburgh, Pennsylvania, becomes the first person ever to get a transplanted heart, liver, and kidney all at once.

MONDAY
December 4

The Soviet Union agrees to supply fuel to the expedition that is trekking across Antarctica, so that the supply plane can keep dropping food for the 6 men and 42 dogs.

TUESDAY
December 5

At a meeting in Pasadena, California, space scientists report that the planet Neptune has 1,500-mile-per-hour winds—the fastest known wind in the whole solar system.

WEDNESDAY
December 6

An 18-foot-long Christmas tree arrives at the White House, in a wagon pulled by two horses named Dick and Fred. The Christmas tree is a gift for the President.

THURSDAY
December 7

Lobzilla, a 21-pound lobster, is set free in the ocean near Portland, Maine. He was rescued from a seafood restaurant in Charlotte, North Carolina.

FRIDAY
December 8

In Richmond, Virginia, a man on the city's "10 most wanted" list is arrested after he shows up at a police station to bail out a friend. His picture was on the wall!

SATURDAY
December 9

The governor of Massachusetts, Michael Dukakis, signs a law today making it illegal to sell assault weapons in Boston.

WHO ELSE WAS BORN IN DECEMBER?
ELI WHITNEY

U.S. inventor

His most famous invention was the cotton gin in 1793, a machine that separated cotton fibers from the cotton seeds. This device changed the entire cotton industry by making cotton-growing much more profitable for farmers.

BORN   December 8, 1765, in Westboro, Massachusetts

SUNDAY
December 10

UN Human Rights Day • An ice storm knocks over a 2,000-foot-tall radio station tower in Auburn, North Carolina.

MONDAY
December 11

The international dog sled team, which set off on August 1 to cross Antarctica, reaches the South Pole today. The 6-person team has traveled 1,900 miles so far.

TUESDAY
December 12

Full Moon

A porcelain horse from the T'ang Dynasty (A.D. 618–907) is sold for $5,900,000 in London, England, a record for Chinese art. The 27-inch horse has a tiny chip in its saddle.

WEDNESDAY
December 13

The Geminid meteor shower can be seen all across the U.S. tonight, with about 50 shooting stars an hour!

THURSDAY
December 14

In Shelton, Connecticut, police officer Michael Fusco revives a dalmatian, using "mouth-to-snout" resuscitation. The dog had passed out after a squash ball became lodged in its throat.
• The Redoubt volcano in Alaska erupts, shooting ash 7 miles in the air.

FRIDAY
December 15

All 4 engines of a jumbo jet shut down when it flies through a cloud of ash and steam from the erupting Redoubt volcano. The plane falls 13,000 feet before the crew can start the engines again.

SATURDAY
December 16

The annual Christmas bird count begins across the U.S. 4,000 volunteers will record bird sightings now through January 3.

TOY BOX '89

Nintendo
Teenage Mutant Ninja Turtles
The dog or cat gumball machine
Riddle Riot
Clever Endeavor
Luva Wool
Flexiblocks
Googolplex
Hypercars

Quickshot Dudley Duck
Barbie (Superstar Barbie, Holiday
   Barbie, Army Barbie)
Betsy Wetsy
Tiny Tears
P.J. Sparkles
Top Christmas Toy **Oopsie Daisy,
a doll that crawls, falls, and cries**

SUNDAY
December 17

A large number of 225,000,000-year-old fossils have been found in Virginia. Some of the species have never been seen before!

MONDAY
December 18

Airlines are forced to ground planes because of the ash from Redoubt volcano in Alaska. • A small earthquake rumbles in Hollister, California.

TUESDAY
December 19

Redoubt volcano subsides. • The premier of Jordan, Mudar Badran, announces the end of martial law, which has been in effect there for 22 years.

WEDNESDAY
December 20

For the third day in a row, part of the Mississippi River is closed because of a 203-mile-long ice jam.

THURSDAY
December 21

Winter solstice • 1,800 pounds of cocaine is seized from a warehouse in Suffolk County, New York. • Pieces of the Berlin Wall are being sold at Bloomingdale's for $12.50 each.

FRIDAY
December 22

Hanukkah begins at sundown. • Worst cold wave since 1985 covers the U.S. east of the Rockies. It's 43°F below 0 in Havre, Montana!

SATURDAY
December 23

Barbie dolls and accessories are selling like hotcakes this Christmas. Barbie has more than 200 accessories. • Santa Claus has a new zip code. It's 30351-1989.

SUNDAY
December 24

Christmas Eve • A huge oil slick slithers toward the Atlantic coast of Morocco after 44,352,000 gallons of crude oil spills from the stricken Iranian tanker *Khark*.

MONDAY
December 25

Christmas • The southern U.S. has its first white Christmas in 100 years; Florida declares a state of emergency because of the snow.

TUESDAY
December 26

At a Christmas party at the Los Angeles Zoo, 2 families of gorillas are treated to popcorn balls, cranberries, rawhide chews, and whole bananas decorated with roses.

WEDNESDAY
December 27

$50,000 worth of soybeans and corn are destroyed when a fire breaks out in a grain storage building in Harris, Iowa.

THURSDAY
December 28

WHALE WATCH IN SOUTHERN CALIFORNIA: The first of 20,000 gray whales are seen swimming south for the winter. Tourists flock to beaches to catch a glimpse of them on their 6,000-mile journey.

FRIDAY
December 29

Playwright Vaclav Havel becomes president of Czechoslovakia—the first noncommunist to be elected for more than 40 years.

SATURDAY
December 30

In the House of Representatives in Washington, D.C., something has been chewing cables and wires inside an office photocopy machine. Attempts to catch the mysterious pest have failed.

SUNDAY
December 31

Full Moon

New Year's Eve. To celebrate, a group of mountain climbers hike up the 14,110-foot Pikes Peak in Colorado and set off firecrackers. • A second is added to the world's clocks to make up for the slowing of the earth's rotation.

PINK-FOOTED GEESE FROM ICELAND EAT ENGLAND'S CARROT CROP

LOTTERY WINNER DONATES MONEY FOR 13-YEAR-OLD'S KIDNEY TRANSPLANT

CHUNK OF THE BERLIN WALL GROUND INTO 1,000 THIMBLES

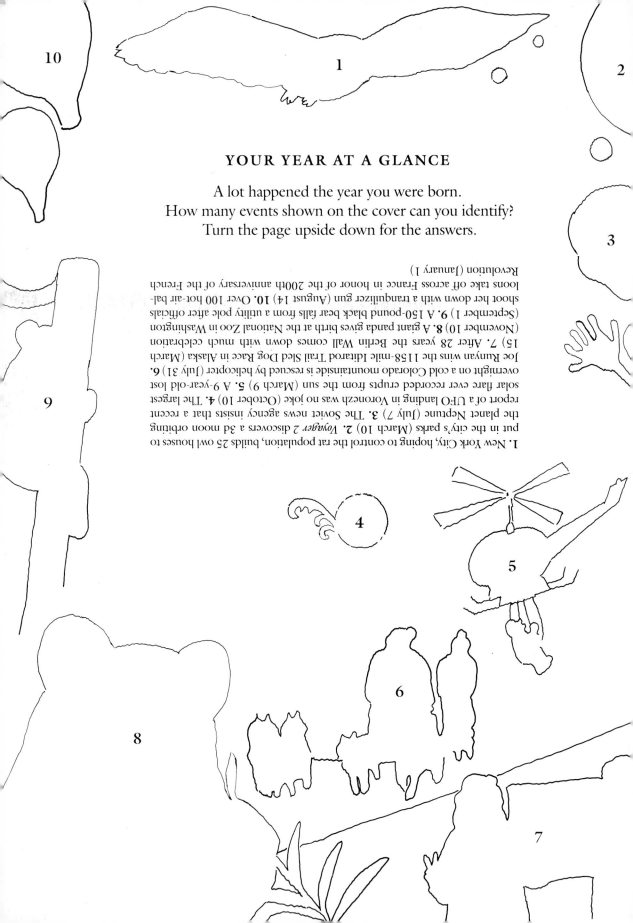

YOUR YEAR AT A GLANCE

A lot happened the year you were born.
How many events shown on the cover can you identify?
Turn the page upside down for the answers.

1. New York City, hoping to control the rat population, builds 25 owl houses to put in the city's parks (March 10) 2. *Voyager 2* discovers a 3d moon orbiting the planet Neptune (July 7) 3. The Soviet news agency insists that a recent report of a UFO landing in Voronezh was no joke (October 10) 4. The largest solar flare ever recorded erupts from the sun (March 9) 5. A 9-year-old lost overnight on a cold Colorado mountainside is rescued by helicopter (July 31) 6. Joe Runyan wins the 1158-mile Iditarod Trail Sled Dog Race in Alaska (March 15) 7. After 28 years the Berlin Wall comes down with much celebration (November 10) 8. A giant panda gives birth at the National Zoo in Washington (September 1) 9. A 150-pound black bear falls from a utility pole after officials shoot her down with a tranquilizer gun (August 14) 10. Over 100 hot-air balloons take off across France in honor of the 200th anniversary of the French Revolution (January 1)